The Student's Quick-Start Guide to Successful Online Learning

Angie Ward, Ph.D.

Ward, Angie
The Student's Quick-Start Guide to Successful Online Learning/Angie Ward

Bite-Sized Books
ISBN: 0615824714
ISBN-13: 978-0615824710

First Edition

Available in print and digital print

Contents

Glossary

CMS Content Management System. A computer program that provides the means for educational participants to create, deliver, edit, and modify components of an online course.

Blended Course A course that utilizes both online and face-to-face delivery of course content.

Distributed Learning A course or educational experience that is held in one or more locations away from the main campus or organization.

Hybrid Course See *Blended Course.*

ILL Inter-Library Loan. A service that allows a patron of one library to borrow materials that are owned by another library.

Intensive Course A course that is delivered on a compressed schedule, e.g. requiring only six to eight weeks compared to a traditional 15-week term.

IT Information Technology.

MOOC Massive Open Online Course. An online course designed for large-scale participation and interaction via the World Wide Web.

VLE Virtual Learning Environment. An educational system that utilizes the World Wide Web to provide virtual access to traditional educational components such as classes, course content, assignments and external resources.

1. INTRODUCTION

Welcome to the Wonderful World of Online Education

Congratulations!

Whether you are currently taking an online class, about to begin a course, or even just contemplating an online program, you are part of a massive trend!

Over the past ten years, enrollment in online academic programs has positively exploded. In 2012, more than seven million students – representing nearly one-third of overall higher-education enrollment -- took at least one online course. That's a ten-year increase of more than *350 percent*. By comparison, traditional higher-education enrollment increased by approximately forty percent over the same period.[1]

These numbers only represent enrollment at higher education institutions. They do not include alternative programs for elementary and secondary students, professional continuing education programs, or "massive open online courses" (MOOC's) such as those offered by Coursera, Udemy and Udacity, which boast enrollments of as many as 40,000 students in one course.[2]

There is no doubt that online education is here to stay. Yet while many organizations are jumping on the online bandwagon, the rapid growth and relative newness of this delivery method mean that there are many uncharted waters and not enough people equipped to navigate them successfully. Traditional institutions, administrators and faculty are struggling to embrace and adapt to the changing face and form of education. While one-third of all higher-education enrollees have taken an online course, "less than one-third of chief academic officers believe that their faculty accept the value and legitimacy of online education."[3]

This is a significant gap. As administrators and teachers struggle through this paradigm shift, the preparation and needs of online students can fall through the cracks. That is why I've written this book.

The purpose of this book is to prepare you for success in your online studies. Whether you are taking just one course or pursuing an entire degree, whether you are a high-schooler, a graduate student or a retired adult learner, whether you are enrolling in an online program at a traditional higher-education institution or exploring a MOOC, this book is designed to explain the unique nature of online education and to equip you to successfully surf these new waters.

My Story

I earned my bachelor's and master's degrees the "old-fashioned" way: by enrolling in, relocating to, and attending class at traditional higher-education institutions. When I was in college, few students had their own computers. By the time I started graduate school a few years later, although I had my own laptop, the Internet was a new (and slow) phenomenon. I remember the excitement of hearing a modem establish an online connection. Some of you are laughing at how primitive we were, while others of you may just now be learning how to get online, albeit without the screeching modem.

Ten years after I earned my master's degree, I was ready to go back to school for my doctorate. However, by this time I was married with two elementary-aged children, and both my husband and I were involved in very fulfilling jobs. Packing up and relocating really was not an option. At the time we lived near a number of major universities so I began to investigate programs in our area. None of them fit what I was really looking for.

One day as I was searching online for options, I came across a guide to distance education programs.[4] I discovered that several reputable schools in my field had recently started online graduate programs that required only brief residencies instead of total relocation. I excitedly requested more information from several schools, made several visits, then a final selection based on conversations with administrators, faculty and alumni. The school I chose allowed me to remain in my job while pursuing my Ph.D. – an option I could never have imagined when I was graduating with my master's degree.

My doctoral program took four and a half years. For the first three years of the program, I made the eight-hour drive from Durham, North Carolina to Louisville, Kentucky two times per year, staying on campus for two weeks at a time but flying home for the intervening weekend. Before and after each residency, I utilized my home computer and the university libraries in my area to complete assigned readings, perform research, write papers, and participate in online discussion forums. During the residencies, my nine-member cohort attended class, submitted papers, made presentations, and conducted additional research. The final year and a half of my program did not require any travel except to defend my dissertation prospectus (proposal) and then the dissertation itself. In December 2011 I was ceremoniously hooded with a fully accredited, fully earned Ph.D. in Leadership. I understand completely what it is like to be a student in an online program.

Meanwhile, during my doctoral studies I was asked to design and teach an online class for undergraduate students at a small private college. That opportunity opened the door to many others over the following years. I have now designed and/or taught more than a dozen online courses from the undergraduate to the doctoral level for a number of institutions, with more invitations each year. Some of these programs were established on a distance model, while others are so new to online education that I am able to teach them as I work with them. All that to say, I also understand completely what it is like to be a course designer and a teacher in an online program.

In addition to studying via a distance program, developing and teaching distance courses, I have written about the options available to adults seeking further education.[5] Based on my conversations, research and experience, I not only understand the options available, I am a vocal advocate for the distance-education model in its various forms.

But most importantly, this book springs from my experience with people like you: the many wonderful students I have been able to teach over the years, whether in a traditional classroom, a hybrid course or an exclusively online context. I learn so much during every course I teach, and one of the things that has been impressed on me throughout my experience is that students desperately need a solid yet easy-to-digest guide to successful online learning.

Purpose and Structure of the Book

I thought about naming this book "Online Learning for Dummies," but: 1) A similar title already exists; 2) By virtue of your entering or even exploring the world of online education, you are certainly no dummy, no matter what level of coursework you undertake. My hope is that this book will be helpful to you whether:

- You are considering an online course or program.

- You have been accepted or enrolled in an online course and are just beginning.

- You are already enrolled in an online course or program but would like better understanding or results in the process.

- You are teaching an online course and would like to direct students to a beneficial resource.

As the title implies, this book is intended as a *quick-start* guide for students embarking on online education. It assumes that you have already researched your options and have a good idea of which course(s) or program you will pursue. It is not a guide to those programs, although hopefully you will find the information helpful if you are still considering your options. As a quick-start guide, the book aims to help you get up and running as fast as possible, not to focus on in-depth discussion of the philosophical and pedagogical pros and cons of online education. In fact, I promise that's the last time I will use the word "pedagogical" in this book.

This book has seven chapters. Chapter One consists of this introduction. Chapter Two, "Changes and Challenges," explores the evolving world of online education so that you can better understand where online education fits in the larger educational context, and its strengths and weaknesses. Chapter Three, "People and Perspectives," introduces you to the parties involved in the online education process and where they're coming from. (There are probably more people involved than you might think!) Chapter Four, "Core Components," covers the common components of an online course so that you can understand the terminology and framework used in all online learning. Chapter Five, "Setting Yourself Up For Success," walks you through the process of getting familiar with a course. Chapter Six, "Procedures and Protocols," addresses critical issues such as pacing, personal discipline, and writing style. Finally, Chapter Seven, "Finding the Help You Need," provides questions and resources to find the answers you need and help you stay on track if you encounter difficulties during your online experience.

If you want to understand the overall context of online education, start with Chapter Two and read on. If you'd rather just dive into your course or program, skip to Chapter Four and forward. And if you're already in a course but you're stuck and don't know where to find help, go directly to Chapter Seven for troubleshooting assistance.

A key feature of this book is that it incorporates the input and insights of dozens of students and professors who have willingly shared what they have learned from their experience with online education. These valuable insights can be found throughout the book in sections titled "Students Speak" or "Professors Speak." Additional wisdom is collected in the Appendix.

Online education has many benefits, as well as many challenges inherent to any new venture. *The Student's Quick-Start Guide to Successful Online Learning* was designed to help you understand and navigate these waters for the most positive experience. Enjoy the journey!

2. CHANGES & CHALLENGES

The Evolving World of Online Education

Online learning exploded onto the educational scene at the turn of the last millennium. In 1996, an entity called "Blackboard Inc." filed a patent for "Internet-based educational support system and methods." The abstract from the application for United States Patent #6,988,138 described the creators' idea:

> A system and methods for implementing education online by providing institutions with the means for allowing the creation of courses to be taken by students online, the courses including assignments, announcements, course materials, chat and whiteboard facilities, and the like, all of which are available to the students over a network such as the Internet. Various levels of functionality are provided through a three-tiered licensing program that suits the needs of the institution offering the program. In addition, an open platform system is provided such that anyone with access to the Internet can create, manage, and offer a course to anyone else with access to the Internet without the need for an affiliation with an institution, thus enabling the virtual classroom to extend worldwide.[1]

Blackboard was soon joined by CourseNotes.com, ePath Learning, CourseWork, and Moodle, among other startups developing online course systems. Virtual learning environments (VLE's) were rapidly gaining interest and steam among students, universities and business corporations. By 2002, more than 1.6 million students at degree-granting higher-education institutions were already taking some type of online course. That number has grown by an average of around 18 percent per year over the last decade, leading to today's online enrollment figure of over seven million students![2]

What Exactly is Online Learning?

It is critical to understand what is meant by the term "online learning." According to the Babson Survey Research Group, there are four typical course classifications, ranging from fully on-campus courses to fully online courses:

1. **Traditional Course** (0% online content). All course content is delivered orally or in writing; no technology is used outside of the classroom.

2. **Web Facilitated Course** (1 to 29% online content). Web-based technology is used to facilitate a face-to-face course. For example, the course may use an online course management system (CMS) to post the syllabus, assignments, and communication from the professor. The majority of on-campus courses today would be classified as Web Facilitated Courses.

3. **Blended or Hybrid Course** (30 to 79% online content). This type of course combines both online and face-to-face delivery. The online component typically includes standard CMS components but will add online discussion and perhaps some content delivery such as video lectures. The need for face-to-face time between teacher and student is reduced by the additional online components. They may be delivered as an "Intensive" or compressed-schedule course, e.g. requiring only six or eight weeks compared to the traditional 15-week term. Blended/Hybrid courses may also be referred to as "Distributed Learning," meaning that the learning is not centralized entirely on-campus.

4. **Online Course** (80% or more online content). In this kind of course, almost all content is delivered online, with few or no face-to-face meetings.[3]

This book focuses on the last two classifications – Blended/Hybrid Courses and Online Courses – and will refer to both of these types of courses as "online learning," and to the first two classifications – Traditional Courses and Web-Facilitated Courses – as "traditional learning." In addition to the classifications above, there are several other important notes about what online learning is and is not.

First, online learning does not necessarily mean "distance" learning. You may live close to an actual campus or even *on* campus and still take an online or hybrid course. However, one of the great benefits of online learning is that it can be delivered around the world to anyone with an

Internet connection. Hybrid courses will also sometimes use local and regional course sites that may be more convenient to the student than the school's main campus.

Second, online learning does not necessarily mean "independent study." Some online courses are indeed self-guided and can be completed at the student's convenience, but an increasing number of online courses require interaction with the professor and/or other students during the course. This interaction must be conducted regularly and by fixed deadlines according to the course schedule.

Third, it is important to understand the difference between an online *course* and an online *program*. While many courses can be conducted entirely online, many academic programs – leading to an accredited certificate or a degree – still require some type of residency requirement, meaning that students must complete a portion of the program on-campus, either via traditional courses or a blended/hybrid format.

The reality is that at the time of this writing, the term "online program" has no standard definition in use by administrators, marketers, professors or even accrediting agencies. A school that advertises, "Earn your degree online!" may be referring to a degree-completion program, a hybrid program, or a fully online program. Therefore, it is important to understand the terminology and to ask what exactly is meant and required by a particular course or program.

Although terms can be confusing, the incredible diversity of online learning is one of its greatest strengths. While some schools may offer only a few online courses, others offer entire degrees with minimal residency requirements that can be satisfied by brief on-campus visits. Class sizes range from two to 20,000 students or more. Reputable and fully accredited online courses and degree programs are now offered at all educational levels including elementary school, middle school, high school, college, and graduate school all the way to terminal degrees such as the doctorate. In addition, corporations, schools and non-profit organizations increasingly offer online courses to provide professional and continuing education programs for non-degree students. The possibilities are nearly endless – which is why this rapidly changing field has also brought challenges to institutions and individuals including administrators, teachers, and students.

The Benefits and Challenges of Online Learning

Online learning has many significant advantages for students:

- **Flexibility:** Students can choose from a variety of courses and programs that suit their particular needs and availability.

- **Affordability:** Online education is often less expensive than traditional programs. Even if the cost per credit is the same as a traditional course, the reduced costs for travel, room and board make online learning an attractive educational option.

- **Opportunity:** This flexibility and affordability mean that thousands, perhaps millions, of students around the world now have unprecedented access to first-rate educational opportunities.

Yet online learning is not without challenges that can affect everyone involved in the process, from individual students to teachers to the entire educational institution.

Students: Although flexibility is a great advantage in online learning, it can also be a significant downfall for some students. Online learning requires internal motivation and discipline. The more independent or advanced the course, the more motivation and self-discipline that are required. Research shows that students in online courses are far more likely to drop a class or quit a program than students in a traditional program.[4]

Students must also recognize that although the delivery method is different and sometimes more flexible, online courses are to deliver the same level of academic rigor as traditional courses. Students who believe that online courses are automatically "easier" are in for a big surprise. The type of work may be different, but the amount and difficulty of work usually are not.

Teachers: Many professors continue to struggle to adapt to online learning as a valid new way of "doing school." They are tied to old educational philosophies and methods, yet are now being asked (or required) to adopt an entirely new paradigm. Online learning presents exciting possibilities for both student and teacher, but designing and teaching an online class requires a completely different approach than preparing for a traditional face-to-face course. Even those who buy into the new method are often asked to add online courses to their existing teaching load. Whether professors are resistant or just overworked, the result is that online courses may not tap into the tremendous potential of this format.

Institutions: Some administrators have seen the vision and potential of technology-based education and are working to change their schools' educational models and policies to incorporate online learning as a key component. Others are adapting more slowly. But at both ends of the spectrum and everywhere in between, I have seen that the pressure of growth and change, whether it is fast or slow, often shows up in the technology department. Marketing departments promote online courses and programs. Professors are contracted to design and teach online offerings. Students sign up by the dozens, the hundreds, even the thousands.

Yet all of this online learning requires significant technological capacity and infrastructure. When the infrastructure can't keep up or breaks down, it impacts course delivery. Students are impacted most immediately and acutely by these failures. Online education mirrors the potential and challenges of the technology on which it is based, and its effectiveness depends on the technological resources allocated by the educational institution.

In addition, the fact that online students may not be physically present on campus means that they can fall through the cracks. While the needs of online students are no less important, administrators and professors may feel more urgency about responding to the students they see on a regular basis. It's generally not personal; it's just a natural consequence of the principle, "Out of sight, out of mind." Still, the frustration for online students is no less palpable, and the challenge persists to provide first-rate service to long-distance and online students.

Navigating the New Frontier

Although the field is already more than ten years old, online education is still a vast new frontier, full of possibility yet not without potential difficulty. The more an online student can understand about this world, its opportunities and challenges, the better prepared he or she will be to navigate this frontier to tremendous personal enjoyment and success. In the next chapter, we will learn more about the key players in this new world.

STUDENTS SPEAK

"The flexibility of the online program is essential. While in my program, my wife and I had our first child, so my schedule was often very hectic as we adjusted to a new way of life. Also, my online program allowed me to interact with people living in different parts of the country and from around the world. The variety of perspectives achieved in an online classroom tends to be far more diverse than just what your local classroom would offer."

"The thing I enjoyed the most was the freedom to study and complete in my own way. Whether that is work environment or schedule, it was freeing to be able to do it on my terms."

"It was hard to stay motivated with my online coursework after being so used to my in-class experience in undergrad. Since I went

straight into the online program from my undergrad program, it was an adjustment to shift from purely in-class learning to online learning.”

PROFESSORS SPEAK

“I have learned that in an online context, it is far more difficult for a student to 'sit-in-the-back-and-disengage.' Whereas that is a definite issue in a residential classroom, every student online must log on and engage.”

“I've noticed that many students take an online class because they think it will be easier. While it may be more convenient, that doesn't mean ease. Here are a few difficulties to anticipate: trips to the library for resources, a large reading workload, working out the logistics of online collaboration, and the unique challenge of communicating effectively online.”

3. PEOPLE AND PERSPECTIVES

Key Players in the World of Online Education

While online learning relies heavily on a virtual environment, there are very real people behind (and in front of) those flickering pixels. As a student, you may be most aware of your online classmates and your professor, but there are actually at least a half-dozen parties with a specific purpose and interest in the process. Many of these roles mirror those you would find on a traditional campus, but their perspectives are applied to an online environment. This chapter introduces you to this cast of characters and their perspectives so that you can understand what happens behind the scenes and navigate successfully your online experience.

Students

Let's start with you – the student in an online course or program. You may be a traditional student in a residential academic program, a high-school student, an adult learner completing an unfinished degree or pursuing a new one while continuing to work and parent full-time, an employee enrolled in mandatory continuing education, a lifelong student who just signed up for a MOOC for personal enrichment, or a retiree taking a class for personal enrichment. Whatever your situation in life, you have the same concerns as any other student: finding time for your studies, managing your social life, balancing your schoolwork with the rest of your activities and responsibilities, and paying for it all without going broke.

You may be taking an online class to finish your program requirements and graduate, so your course may look almost like an independent study that supplements or completes your on-campus program. Or you may be pursuing an entire degree as a full-time online student; for you, this *is* school.

Speaking of school: you want to get good grades, sure, but at some level you also want to enjoy the process. (Adult learners especially want to learn all they can and not just jump through hoops to get a certificate or degree.) You want to feel supported and valued, especially in a class or program you care about or are interested in. You don't want to get lost in the shuffle.

To be successful, an online student's primary need is *communication*: communication from the school or organization about the entire learning process (application, enrollment, registration, navigating the school and course web sites, where to find help); and communication from the professor about course requirements and expectations, and how to contact him or her if needed. A student also needs communication in the form of regular feedback about progress in the course. This includes updated information about grades received, and timely and detailed feedback on assignments such as papers and projects.

In a physical campus environment, students can just walk over to the appropriate university office between classes or to the professor's office during open hours and find answers to their questions. In an online environment, every party must seek to *over*-communicate to make up for this loss of face-to-face interaction.

Teachers

I lump "teachers" together in one category, but the reality is that there are many different types and levels of teachers, especially in a college or university environment. There are professional and corporate trainers. There are instructors and professors with ranks such as "Junior," "Adjunct," "Associate," "Senior," or "Emeritus" attached to their titles. Some teachers specialize exclusively in online classes. Some are adjuncts (supplementary teachers, usually part-time) or freelancers, either for the flexibility it provides or for the opportunity to get a foot in the door to the ivory tower. Others are fully tenured, on-campus professors who have been assigned an online course. Some teachers wrote or designed the course they are teaching; others are "teaching" (or, really, facilitating) someone else's content.

Just as there is great variation in each teacher's situation, there is great variation in the attitudes of teachers toward online learning. Some of my colleagues grumble that online learning is bad for education. That, of course, depends on one's definition of education. If "education" refers only to traditional, face-to-face classroom instruction that relies heavily on a lecture format, then yes, online learning is "bad" for education in that it challenges an age-old model. Many professors continue to struggle to adapt to online learning as a new way of "doing school." This can reflect a particular educational philosophy or general resistance to doing something differently. Sometimes it even reflects insecurity: about their own teaching ability or about their job security in such a rapidly changing educational environment compounded by institutional budget cuts.

On the other hand, I have met and worked with many teachers who believe that online learning is not only a viable educational option – it is the way of the future, and the best way at that. These professors are experimenting with and capitalizing on new teaching methods and tools that were unavailable to previous generations of educators. They view online teaching as an opportunity, not a chore, even if it is hard work. My hope is that you will have the opportunity to learn from some of these fine colleagues.

Online instructors often face a steep learning curve. They must adapt their course content and teaching style to an online or hybrid format and they often must learn new technological platforms to be able to interact with students in the course. Some schools utilize professional help to develop the online course web site, while some schools expect teachers to set it up themselves.

Like students, teachers need *communication*. They need communication from their institution, and that communication must come from several departments, as we will see shortly. Teachers also need communication from their students. Just as in a face-to-face class, teachers want to know what is working and not working, which material is causing difficulty for students, and if there are any other student concerns that might affect participation and performance in class.

Teachers also need *support* from the administration. Teachers want to know that that they will be respected as professionals, that they will be allowed to teach and manage their classes in the way they deem best, and that the administration will "have their back" if they come under fire.

Course Designers

In many instances, teachers design the online courses that they teach. In some situations, however, one individual or group may design the course while another may teach it. For example, a full-time professor may create, design, and teach a course the first time it is offered, but a part-time instructor may be hired to "teach" the course materials in subsequent semesters. As you can imagine, there are multiple opportunities for miscommunication with this system, as instructors are expected to "teach" a course they did not design and content with which they are not very familiar.

Academic Administration

Educational institutions are complex organizations. Even small colleges and training schools have multiple branches, and multiple departments within each branch. An online teacher will generally report to some type of academic administrator, such as a department chair or dean. Academic administrators are charged with protecting the academic integrity of the institution. This means that they are concerned with the type and quality of courses that are offered, how they fit into an overall program of study, and whether they pass muster with whatever outside organization(s) provide accreditation to their organization. Accreditation is a big deal, as it provides external endorsement of the school's quality and trustworthiness. It is also used by federal and local government agencies to determine qualification for financial support, including student aid programs.

Academic administrators must also oversee the faculty. In some cases, administrators protect them (for example, approving and supporting tenure), and in other cases they challenge professors to growth and accountability (for example, making sure that a class meets accreditation standards). This is not to say that academic administrators are not concerned about the individual student, but that they have multiple interests and responsibilities that can sometimes conflict with each other. Their relationship with students is manifest through administration of academic records and recognition and verification of student progress in the chosen course or program.

The primary need for academic administration is *compliance*, in the sense that they maintain academic standards and all parties under their oversight must comply with those standards. Students are expected to follow course and program protocols. Teachers are expected to follow accrediting standards and best educational practices in their design and delivery of courses. And the academic administration itself is expected to ensure that its department complies with the standards prescribed by their supervisors and reviewers.

Support Services

In addition to academic administration, educational organizations require support services. These individuals or departments support the educational mission of the organization, although some academic types will note that it feels as though academics have become the appetizer instead of the entrée on the institutional menu. Nevertheless, support services are charged with helping make the academic side "happen" by enhancing the student experience. For an online student, the entities most commonly encountered include the marketing/admissions/enrollment department(s), student affairs, and the information technology department.

The mission of each department is generally clear from its title. Marketing folks spread the word about the organization and its programs. Admissions departments turn interest into applications and enrollments. Student affairs encompasses a broad spectrum of services and programs that enhance the student's overall learning and development. These could include student housing, residence life, campus safety, multicultural affairs, health services and recreational programs, and even the campus bookstore, to name just a few of the dozens of possibilities. And of course, the information technology (IT) department is responsible for the development, maintenance and support of the organization's technological resources and services.

Students in online programs will generally interact with fewer departments and programs than a traditional student. Many schools are still working to determine what types of student services to provide to online students and how best to provide them. In many cases, an online student will engage with student services offices primarily at the beginning of their time with the school as they enroll, receive initial academic advising, and obtain a student I.D. card.

The one exception to this general principle is the IT department and in particular, technical support. Online learning, of course, depends on the school's web-based resources. If you can't access the course web site, you can't listen to a lecture, contribute to the class discussion, or submit an assignment. If you can't log in to the school's online library, you can't access the research and resources you need for your coursework. The nature of online learning makes effective technological services critical to the success of each student, of each course, and of the overall program.

IT truly wants to help you, but may be under-resourced. In some cases, they may not understand how online education fits into the overall purpose and programs of the organization, or they may not understand their role and relationship with an online student. IT may be focused – or directed to focus – its work on the needs of traditional students. Therefore, these departments may need to learn about their online students' needs. Fortunately, the landscape is changing as more organizations adopt online learning opportunities. Some IT departments are actually leading the way for those organizations. The good examples are doing their jobs to the best of their abilities as they also adapt to a changing educational paradigm.

External Parties

In addition to the entities within an organization, there are several parties outside of the institution that have an interest in online learning programs.

Accrediting Agencies

The most significant of these is accrediting agencies. These are regional or national agencies that evaluate a school and determine whether the education provided by the institution meets acceptable levels of quality. While the U.S. Department of Education does not accredit educational institutions or programs, the Secretary of Education recognizes and relies on the evaluations of private and state agencies to determine a school's eligibility for government funding programs, including financial aid.[1] In addition, other institutions rely on accreditation when determining whether to grant admission or transfer credit.

Accreditation is a big deal. The review process is rigorous, generally conducted every five to ten years. It includes an institutional self-review, followed by an in-depth review by an institution's peers within the accrediting agency. If your organization is preparing for or undergoing accreditation review, you might find administrators to be especially stressed.

The advent of online education has intensified the pressure felt by all parties during the review process.

Academic review used to be a fairly standard process with standard criteria, but online learning has introduced new factors into the process. Reviewers want to make sure that online courses and programs provide the same level of academic rigor as traditional courses. Many educational programs have traditionally required a residency component, as the face-to-face classroom experience has been viewed as a critical component of the overall educational experience. Therefore, accrediting agencies want to ensure that online courses provide a similar level of class interaction. Some agencies have been faster to recognize the changing landscape and the possibilities of online learning. Others have stuck to a more traditional interpretation of standards during their review process.

It's important to understand the tensions and difficult questions that online learning has introduced at the accreditation level. These tensions have trickled down to educational organizations as every party adjusts to the changing landscape. Many schools want to offer flexible online programs, yet some accrediting agencies require more structure. It is also important to understand that accrediting agencies differ in their acceptance and opinion of online educational options. Therefore, a school accredited by one agency may be able to offer a master's degree with little to no residency requirement. Another school, under a different agency, may only be able to allow one-third of the courses in a master's degree to be completed online.

Third-Party Providers

The final entity in the world of online education is third-party providers. These are individuals or companies that are hired by the educational organization to design or manage their online learning. They can range from freelance writers who are paid to design a new online course to large educational companies that focus exclusively on online learning and are contracted to handle a school's entire online educational program. These third-party providers may work with academic administration, faculty, and IT to fulfill their responsibilities. They bring expertise that can be very helpful to a school, but they can also bring an additional layer of bureaucracy that requires additional communication and can still result in significant frustration.

For example, a school may ask a current faculty member to turn an existing, face-to-face class into an online course. The faculty member might create the course using the school's standard syllabus template. However, the external course-design company, which may employ non-educators in the design process, might require significant additional documentation that explains the syllabus and how the components of the course fit together. The partner entity would then use this information to format the course on the web. Finally, it would hand management of the completed course back to the institution's IT department and the teacher.

In theory, this can streamline the system and allow each entity to focus on its strengths. In reality, my experience and observation has so far shown that this system results in extra work for all parties. Teachers get frustrated by the additional work required, often much more than for a traditional course. (In addition, turning a face-to-face course into an effective online course usually requires a complete re-design and not just "simple" tweaks, as the different delivery method also dictates the use of different teaching methods.) Meanwhile, IT professionals find themselves dealing with a third party who may not understand their particular infrastructure – yet they are left to trouble-shoot and fix problems once the course is up and running.

The Business Office

Of course, there is also a financial component to all of this. Online education can be a cash cow for an organization, as it does not require a bricks-and-mortar campus or its related services and maintenance. Teachers and students can be located anywhere in the world, as long as they can access the Internet to connect with each other via the course's technological infrastructure. Once an online course is designed, it can be used for several semesters or even several years; each use of the same course brings increasing profit on the initial expense. Plus the majority of the process, from course design to teaching and grading, can be outsourced, potentially leading to dramatically lower costs for in-house staff salaries and benefits.

Add these financial advantages to the benefits that online learning provides for students and it is no wonder that online education has exploded over the last decade. But as with any business, it is critical that delivery (a pleasant, worthwhile student experience) is able to keep up with sales (marketing, admissions and enrollment). The change in educational paradigm also requires a shift in organizational financial strategy and budgeting. Business offices need their organizations to cover their operating expenses, and the nature and source of these expenses has changed as the educational landscape has changed.

Playing Well With Others

As you can see, there are many players in the world of online learning – perhaps many more than you had considered before this chapter. Each party has its own perspective and priorities. Unfortunately, students can sometimes feel the effects of miscommunication or misalignment of values between these parties. As the field of online education continues to develop, it is my hope and trust that many of these bumps will be solved or at least smoothed over, resulting in a first-rate, enjoyable experience for everyone involved.

4. CORE COMPONENTS

The Common Elements of an Online Course

Now that we've explored a bit of the history and current landscape of online education, let's dive into the actual environment of an online class.

Each school utilizes some type of online "platform" – an online "environment" utilized by the school to host all of the components necessary for an online course. Most schools and organizations utilize one of several common platforms that is customized with the school's logo and other layout and design elements to provide a unique experience for students at that institution. Common platforms currently include Blackboard, Moodle/Joule, Sakai and Udemy.

Every component of a traditional class has a counterpart in the online environment. Lectures, syllabi, discussions, assignments, tests – all can be part of the online learning experience just as they can be used in a traditional classroom environment.

Course Content

In an online course, the content is usually arranged visually in blocks or "units," with each unit generally representing one week of the course. Since online courses can be re-used for multiple class terms, you will need to look carefully for the dates for each unit and for assignment deadlines, as they may be posted separately from the original course documents. Within each unit, you will find various components relevant to that week's topic and assignments.

Course Components
Traditional vs. Online

Traditional Component	Online Counterpart
Live lecture	Video or audio lecture
Assigned reading	Assigned reading
Class discussion (verbal)	Class discussion (written)
Papers submitted in-class or online	Papers submitted in-class (hybrid) or online
Presentations	Difficult in an online context but students may be required to submit video files or links
Tests & Quizzes	Online interactive assessments or an actual test administered and supervised by a third-party "proctor"
Library	Online library access, local libraries or Inter-Library Loan (ILL)

Lectures

In an online course, lectures are delivered via video or audio files. Video or audio may be embedded directly into the course unit and accessed by just clicking the "play" button, or it may be provided via a link the student must click to access the file in another location, such as YouTube.

Professors can record video lectures in several ways. They may record a live classroom presentation or seminar for use in an online course, or they may speak to a video camera in a studio, office or classroom. Whereas a professor in the classroom may lecture for 30 minutes to an hour or more at one time, lectures for an online course are usually divided into smaller chunks of no more than 15 minutes. This allows online students to navigate the material more easily and to take breaks, if needed.

Slide Shows

Just as in a traditional classroom, an online instructor may supplement a lecture with a slide show. Slide shows can be embedded with the lecture or provided as a video, a PowerPoint or Keynote file, or a link. For example, one professor might record herself speaking as the "soundtrack" to a PowerPoint slide show. Another instructor might appear in a video, speaking while the slide show is projected next to him. Still another might require students to click through a PowerPoint show themselves while listening to an audio file of the lecture. The delivery method will depend on the format that is preferred and supported by the school and its technological capabilities.

Handouts

Online instructors may also provide "handouts" such as the course syllabus, lecture notes, diagrams, outlines and assignment guidelines. These may be downloadable resources including Word, Excel, photo or PDF files; they may be accessed via a link that opens the file in the student's web browser; or a combination of both. Again, the delivery method for these supplemental materials will depend on the preferences and capabilities of the instructor or the institution.

Class Discussion

In-class discussion is a key component of many traditional courses. Online courses also offer students the opportunity to interact with their classmates via discussion forums. Frequently, an instructor will pose discussion-starting questions based on a unit's content, readings and concepts. Students must then compose and post a thoughtful response to the question. Many courses also require responses to the posts of others in the class.

Although these discussions are not "live" as in a chat room or on instant messaging, they do create an online "conversation" among class members and provide a way for students to interact with the materials presented in the course. To facilitate timely, ongoing discussion, the professor will often specify regular short-term deadlines for each contribution.

Many online learning platforms also provide an out-of-class "hangout" area where students can connect to share notes, form study groups, or gripe about the class. In other words, it's just like a lounge at a traditional school. In addition, you can get to know your classmates by looking at the personal profiles they have set up on the course site.

Assignments

Whether you are taking a traditional class or an online course, you can expect the professor to give a variety of assignments, including readings, papers and projects. In an online course, most of this work takes place offline, although it is usually submitted to the professor via the course web site.

Readings can include sections from required textbooks, as well as articles or web sites. Some readings may be provided on the course site, while others, as in a traditional classroom, require a student to purchase the book, borrow it from the library, or find the resource on the Internet.

Papers are completed outside of class and submitted according to the professor's preference or the school's protocol. Some professors prefer to use editing capabilities in Microsoft Word and will request that papers be submitted as a Word document. Others may request PDF files, while a few may still require students to mail them a hard copy. The submission format will determine how a professor grades and returns your work. Some instructors will "track changes" directly in the document or use a stylus to mark a PDF document digitally, then send the attachment back to the student electronically. Others will print a hard copy of the electronic file, mark it by hand, and return via snail mail.

Projects depend on the nature of the course, the delivery method (online or hybrid), the preferences of the instructor, and the capabilities of the school's online platform. Professors of hybrid courses often require students to bring completed projects with them to campus. Online instructors may require online or hard copy submission of audio or video files or documents from multiple parties as part of a group project. For example, I once taught an online Teaching Practicum course that required students to submit a video teaching sample, along with evaluation forms from peers and mentors. Another course required students to submit an online portfolio as a capstone project for their undergraduate major. Online course designers definitely require a certain degree of creativity to provide meaningful project experiences similar to what a student would undertake in a traditional course.

Tests

Tests are another course component requiring some creativity and flexibility in an online environment. Many online learning platforms now offer the capability to administer online quizzes and quantitative assessments. However, it is more difficult to control the testing environment, as online students obviously do not come together into one classroom where access to resources (e.g. cheat notes and open books) can be limited.

There are several methods for administering tests to students in an online course. One approach is to allow open books/open notes during an assessment, whether an online quiz or a longer essay test that is submitted electronically. Another is to require students to take the test under the supervision of a proctor: an adult who is present with the student during the test, and signs an affidavit that the student completed the test without outside assistance or resources.

Research

The majority of courses for academic credit will require some type of outside research. The higher the level of education, the more likely the course will require advanced, independent research. In a traditional course, students can simply walk over to the on-campus library to conduct this research. In an online course, students must learn other research methods and strategies to complete the work required. Fortunately, the technological developments that led to the explosive growth of online education have been accompanied by similar advances in the field of library science.

All academic libraries now provide at least some of their resources and materials online. At the very least, online catalogs allow students to search and compile lists of materials from their computer, saving time once they visit the physical library to access these items. However, most libraries now also provide a rich array of services and resources that a student can access entirely online. From theses and dissertations to full-text articles to digitized archive materials to entire books, students can often access everything they need from the comfort of their own desk. Students can contact librarians via telephone, email and instant chat, and some libraries even hire staff for the exclusive service of online students. In addition, Inter Library Loan (ILL) allows patrons to request books and other materials from participating libraries all over the world.

Schools with online programs often provide tutorials on the use of the institution's library services. Many online programs also require new students to establish borrowing privileges at the nearest research library, and to demonstrate the ability to utilize online research resources.

Calendar

Somewhere on the course web site you will find a visual calendar. You may find that some dates are highlighted: perhaps circled, bold-faced, or perhaps in another color. Pay special attention to highlighted dates, as they represent significant events or deadlines that correspond with assignments outlined in the course syllabus.

Gradebook

Students in online courses can view their grades in the course's online gradebook. The "grades" section of the course site will list all assignments, along with maximum points or percentages as part of the final grade. Unlike traditional courses where a student may not know a final grade until the end of the course term, students in courses with an online gradebook can monitor their progress as often as the professor updates the grades.

Online courses aim, as much as possible, to provide everything a student would experience in an on-campus environment. While the online format has some limitations, in many areas online learning offers opportunities for innovation and improvement on the traditional course experience. But one similarity between on-campus and online programs is that it still takes time for new students to gain familiarity with their surroundings and to figure out the best strategies for their own success. The next chapter explains how to set yourself up for a most successful and enjoyable online learning experience.

PROFESSORS SPEAK

"Research, at least in the humanities, can still be done almost as successfully online, IF libraries make key books or key parts of books available online via scanned copy, if students have access to electronic databases with recent articles and book chapters in full PDF format, and if they can access a live academic library for at least a short period of time."

5. SETTING YOURSELF UP FOR SUCCESS

Getting Up and Running in an Online Course

You've taken the plunge. You've applied, been accepted, and registered for your first online course. Now what?

Get Connected

First things first: If you haven't already done so, it's time to make sure your technology is up to the task. A positive online learning experience begins with your ability to quickly and reliable access the course via the Internet. Quick and reliable access begins with an up-to-date computer that can handle the tremendous amount of data processing required by today's graphic interfaces – the stuff you see on your screen. You may have a blazing fast Internet connection, but if your computer has a slow processor, you may still be frustrated by slow loading and uploading times. This doesn't mean you need to go out and buy a new computer, although many students find that the beginning of an online program is the perfect time to upgrade. However, if your computer is more than three or four years old, you should at least look into upgrading, if not replacing, your current system.

Either a desktop or laptop computer will work great for an online course. However, be sure to do some research before going with a tablet device such as an iPad. First, the tablet's keyboard may slow your typing, or you may need to add an external keyboard. Second, but more importantly, many online platforms are not yet fully compatible with tablet operating systems (OS). In my opinion and experience, tablets are more suitable for students in MOOC's or professional development courses that require less writing and typing than a typical course for full academic credit. Check with your particular school or organization to learn whether their online platform is fully compatible with tablet computers.

Next, you need to secure a connection to the Internet. Fortunately, most students can easily make this connection, either at home via service from a local telephone, cable, or satellite provider, or via WiFi (wireless) access at any number of public places including schools, libraries, coffee shops, and restaurants. The key is that your connection must be both *reliable* and *available*. *Reliable* means that the connection remains steady so that you can get and remain online. *Available* means that you can gain access when you need it. For example, you may be traveling abroad and planning to use Internet cafés to check in with your class. That's great, as long as you can get online during the days and times specified in the syllabus to access course content, contribute to class discussions, and submit assignments.

Get Organized

After you've determined that your technology passes muster, set up a good calendar. You may decide to use the calendar or a task list on your smart phone, or you may decide to keep a separate, paper or computer-based calendar for your coursework. Either system is fine, as long as you can use it to record all of your school obligations in one place.

The course platform may include a calendar with major due dates, and the professor will likely post a syllabus; however, it's still best to transfer all that information to one calendar that you can access easily and regularly, and that allows you to see all your assignments and due dates from all classes at one glance. Include deadlines for online discussion contributions as well as major assignments and assessments. One of my biggest frustrations as a professor (in any format, actually) is students who don't closely read and follow the syllabus, therefore missing details and deadlines. Help yourself by setting up an organizational system that works for you.

This is especially important for adult learners who are balancing school with the demands of family and full-time work. Having all of your commitments, due dates and deadlines in one place will help you see where you might need to work ahead or work around competing activities, and give you an idea of how the rhythm of school fits with the rest of your life.

In addition to a comprehensive calendar, you should create one area (such as a drawer, file, folder, or notebook) where you keep all of your login information for the course site and other departments or resources including the library, student services, student accounting/financial aid, registrar, etc. This file should also contain contact information for the course instructor and for the technical support department.

Get Familiar

Next, spend some concentrated time exploring the course site and overall online platform. Some schools may provide written or online tutorials, but don't be afraid to click around on your own as well. Familiarize yourself with the process for logging in and finding the course site. Once you're logged in, you will see your "Dashboard." This is the main "landing" or entry page where you will find general news and information from your school or organization, as well as links to offices, relevant resources, and all of your courses.

From here, click to enter a course and look for the areas described below. (Note: Not every platform, school or course will include all of these features and they may have different names, but attempt to locate as many as possible.)

- **Course Calendar.** This will have due dates and other important school deadlines such as course add/drop deadlines, exam dates, and final grade deadlines.

- **Latest News.** As the title suggests, this section, often located in the sidebar (in a column to the left or right of the page), contains updates and information relevant to your course.

- **Upcoming Assignments.** Whereas the course calendar gives you an overview of all due dates, the Upcoming Assignments (or Events) section, lists the next important assignments or dates in the course.

- **Syllabus.** Locate the course syllabus and any other introductory information or resources. These may be downloadable hard copies, audio/video files, or links to relevant pages.

- **Course Units.** Your course will be divided into units or weeks. Each unit section will include links and files for content and resources pertaining to that unit's topic.

- **Discussion Area or Forum.** You may find this under particular units in the course, or it may be a separate area that you can see no matter what unit you are working on.

- **Assignment Submission.** Find out where and how you are to submit assignments for this course. Does the instructor specify a particular type of file, such as a Word document or a PDF? Are you to email the assignment to the professor, or upload it to a particular section on the course site?

- **Grades.** Click on this link to see a list of assignments for your course and, if completed, the grade you received.

- **Participants.** Use this link to see who else is in your class and find out more about them, based on what they have entered in their personal profile.

- **Your Profile.** Look for your own profile and take some time to edit your photo and personal information. Make sure that your contact information is correct.

- **Settings.** Browse this section to see what settings have been assigned for your course and to make changes if desired. For example, most online platforms allow you to choose between receiving an email every time there is a new discussion post, or receiving one summary email per day.

- **Contact Information.** Look for the instructor's contact information. This may be found on his/her profile in the "Participants" section, and/or on the course syllabus. Also look for information about how to contact technical support. Write this information on your calendar or another piece of paper and store in a safe place so you will have it if you are unable to access the course online.

- **Library and Research Tools.** You may find a link from your course site, or you may need to access these resources separately, depending on your institution or program. Make sure you know how to log on to whatever online research sites you will be using for your course.

Once you have located these areas on your course site, bookmark the site and the addresses of other resource sites such as the library, so that you can easily access them in the future.

Congratulations on navigating your way through an online course site! Now that you are up and running, the next chapter will look at the best practices for your best success as a student in an online course.

STUDENTS SPEAK

"I would tell a new distance education student that they should approach online education with a working knowledge of their own learning style. If they learn best by absorbing as much information as possible then it is best to take a lighter load of courses and concentrate on fewer subjects. If they learn best through a "fire hose" learning environment or work best with lots to do, then take more courses. But I would advise all online ed students to start light and work their way up so to avoid wasting time, money, and potential learning opportunities."

"A major key to success in my online learning experience was to factor in class work as a part of my work schedule. I literally marked my calendar with time slots dedicated to my class requirements."

PROFESSORS SPEAK

"Get to know the school's portal for online courses like the back of your hand."

"Know the technology requirements for your course, especially plugins and bandwidth."

"Get familiar with instructional technology terms if you are new to online instruction. There are many glossaries out there."

"Set up an organizational strategy for your email — categorize them in an email folder by week/session of the course."

6. PROCEDURES AND PROTOCOLS

A Professor's Tips for Maximum Success

This is the part of the book where I put on my "professor hat."

Instructors, especially those who are full-time professors in traditional environments, make a lot of assumptions about what their students understand about academic procedures and protocols. Professors live in an academic environment all the time and assume that others are equally familiar with it. However, my experience with online education has shown that students in online courses need specific guidelines and reminders about what is expected in an academic setting.

The purpose of this chapter is to explain, from a professor's perspective, what you need to know to succeed in your course or program. The skills and habits you develop during your online studies will prove useful not only for your academic career, but for your professional and personal life as well. In particular, we will look at what it means to be part of an academic community; how to write and read for academic success; and how to develop the discipline needed to succeed in the online classroom and beyond.

Joining the Academic Community

Whether you are undertaking a full-fledged degree program, earning continuing education credit, or just taking a class for personal enrichment, and whether you are a 19-year-old undergraduate or a 58-year-old doctoral student: by enrolling in an online course, you become part of an academic community. And both words in the term "academic community" come with significant expectations and implications.

Academic

It is important to remember that although you are pursuing your education via an electronic delivery format, you are still part of an *academic* community, and this type of community has particular standards and expectations for its members. For example, you will be expected to tailor your course-related writing and other communication to an academic audience. In addition, you will be subject to the academic world's protocols, and your institution's policies regarding intellectual property and plagiarism. We will look more closely at writing for an academic audience in the next section of this chapter.

Community

As an online student you become part of an academic *community*. Like any community, the academic community has a particular structure and hierarchy and specific (although not always spoken) expectations about how its members should interact with each other. In particular, you will be expected to be respectful of instructors, administrators and fellow learners, both in your specific course or program and in the academic community at large. This respect is demonstrated in the ways you communicate with these people in person, in writing and online, and in the proper credit you give to the work of others. You will also need to remember that. even though you may be located thousands of miles from the main institution, you are still a representative of that institution as a student and later as an alumnus.

Membership in this community has certain responsibilities, but it also brings significant benefits. Even if you never meet your classmates in person, you will be surprised at the close bonds that can develop through your online interaction. Students in online environments become adept at connecting via electronic communication and social media, and those connections can be just as real and as deep as in-person relationships. In addition, because online students may connect from all over the world, there is opportunity for broader networking than may occur on a localized, physical campus.

During my four-and-a-half year doctoral program, which utilized a hybrid format, I heard many comments from residential students that they were envious of the close bonds that formed in my nine-member cohort. Because our interaction had to be more focused both online and on-campus, we developed deep friendships and working relationships that continue to this day. Through my online connections there and in other schools, I have gained dozens of new friends, colleagues, and professional opportunities around the country.

STUDENTS SPEAK

"I really enjoyed the experience and expertise from the variety of course instructors. Many of the professors had many years of experience in their field and brought that experience to the online ed. arena. This was possible because of the freedom and convenience of online teaching. If we were tied to a classroom setting, then I would imagine many of those professors would not have the time to teach in-class sessions."

"I wish I had known how critical relationships are to higher education. The content of the classes is incredibly beneficial to a student; the process of education and meeting deadlines helps students develop; but the relationships built while in school – even online – are by far the best and most crucial element to education. It becomes your network after you've graduated."

"Read your books early, slowly, and take notes. Work hard toward synthesis of assigned texts. Reserve judgments about the applicability of texts until the end of the course. Be prepared to learn from others and be open to see parts of yourself—even the ugly ones—through the studies."

"Find someone else to share the journey with. That is, a person you can e-mail from time to time for encouragement, to answer questions on assignments, and to encourage you. This one was a HUGE part of the journey for me."

"Call and email your fellow students and your profs a lot. Your professors are there to train you, encourage you, equip you, and sometimes exhort you. The camaraderie you develop with your peers is your icing on the cake, your steak and potatoes, and often your lifeline. In short, work hard to develop relationships in person and over the airwaves."

PROFESSORS SPEAK

"I have witnessed two extremes in this area of social 'presence.' Some students interact with hard facts and content, and offer little emotional-social contribution. The other extreme is the absence of social 'filters' that encourages some students to 'dump' their emotional baggage on the rest of the class. There seems to be a sense of 'safety' in writing something on their computer that they would probably not state verbally to others in a face-to-face context. I seek to draw more out of students in the first category and remind students in the second category that the web/email is not as 'private' as they might assume."

Writing (and Reading) for an Academic Environment

One of the most difficult transitions that I have observed among new online students is the transition to writing effectively for an academic audience. As a student in an online program, you will be writing for several formats and audiences: communication with instructors and school administrators, communication with your classmates, online course discussions, and assignments and papers. The majority of these formats require a formal writing style. However, for most new students, their previous online communication has primarily utilized informal communication methods such as emails, Facebook and Twitter posts, online messaging, and text messages.

But just because a course is delivered online does not mean that you can use an informal writing style. An online course discussion forum is still an academic environment, and you must structure your writing for it as you would for a scholarly paper. Good academic writing will demonstrate the following characteristics:

- Your overall writing style should be formal, not casual. You do not need to use "thee" and "thou," but you should write as though you do not have a personal relationship with your reader.

- For papers and assignments, write using third-person perspective. Do not use "I" or "you" in academic writing.

- Support your assertions. There is no place in academic writing for sermonizing or pontificating. If you write, "The world is going to hell in a hand basket," be prepared to back up your assertion with reputable research and hard data.

- Document your sources. All ideas, words and phrases that are not your own must be properly cited and credited to the originator. Your writing should always include the answer to the question, "Says who?"

- Use complete sentences, not phrases or fragments. Formal writing is different from the conversational style you might use in an email to a friend.

- Use real words, not slang or abbreviations. Academic writing should not read like a text message.

- Never use emoticons in formal academic writing, and avoid all other "Netspeak" such as abbreviations. Keep your LOL's to your personal life.

- Always begin by addressing your instructor with his or her professional title, such as "Dr." or "Professor." Do not assume a first-name basis; let the instructor communicate his or her preference if different from the formal title.

- Official communication, even via email, should be written in appropriate business letter or memo format with the proper headings, salutation, sentence and paragraph structure, and closing.

- Contributions to online discussions, even rebuttals to other students' posts, should always be respectful. At its best, the academic community should be a safe place for intellectual inquiry and thoughtful dialogue. No bullying, name-calling, or angry screeds of the type of you might find in a passionate online sports discussion board.

For more specific guidelines, consult the style manual recommended by your professor or provided by your school. Common guides include *The Chicago Manual of Style*, the various MLA style manuals, Kate Turabian's *A Manual for Writers of Research Papers, Theses and Dissertations,* and *The Publication Manual of the American Psychological Association.* You should also check to see if your institution has a writing center that can help you improve your academic writing.

(You will note that this book is *not* written in formal academic style.)

In addition to developing as a writer, you may need to improve your reading skills. At the graduate level in particular, online courses require a lot of reading, often more than may be required for a traditional class. You will greatly increase your odds of success if you are able to read and digest material quickly. A classic tool to increase your skill in this area is *How to Read a Book: The Classic Guide to Intelligent Reading* by Mortimer Adler and Charles Van Doren. You can also search the Internet for various speed-reading books and courses.

STUDENTS SPEAK

"The tone and tenor of the online forums is NOT like Facebook, where you chat, post pictures, and generally waste time. Online forums are purely academic in nature and, depending on the professor, may require the same APA or MLA writing requirements as your in-class counterpart."

"When posting, quality is more important than quantity, and simplicity more than complexity."

"In my experience, online courses typically compensate for hours in the classroom with double the amount of reading, research, and paper writing. If you're a slow reader, like I am, consider getting audio books or setting your Kindle to read to you. Bottom line, keep up with your reading."

"In my opinion, the key to success in an online program is to not shut down one's mind when one walks away from the material. One must be constantly thinking about the work in order to process the content when away from the computer."

PROFESSORS SPEAK

"In a class or program that includes research paper(s), it would be helpful for students to understand what a research paper is — that it's not just regurgitating facts, but that the writer uses data collected and critical thinking to answer a question or solve a problem. It's amazing how many students do not understand this."

"Practice your keyboarding skills."

"Never copy and paste from a website without citation. It is as easy for instructors to catch plagiarism as it was for you to copy/paste in the first place."

Developing the Self-Discipline to Succeed

It is usually a lack of self-discipline, and not the difficulty of the schoolwork itself, that causes students to struggle in online courses. Of course this is true in even traditional learning environments, but the particular freedom and flexibility of an online learning environment – its greatest assets – can also present greater challenges. Students who do not possess or quickly learn critical self-discipline skills will struggle to meet deadlines, manage the many components of an online course, and balance schoolwork with other commitments.

In addition, a traditional class generally incorporates regular attendance as a means for student accountability. By contrast, the lack of a physical classroom in online courses, coupled with the flexibility of the delivery method, often results in an "out of sight, out of mind" effect that makes it easy for students to fall behind.

In addition to setting up a comprehensive calendar as discussed in Chapter 5, here is the counsel I give all online students:

- **Make school a priority.** This may sound like a no-brainer, but I am surprised by how many students think school is a secondary (or lower) commitment to the rest of their life's activities, including but not limited to family vacations, home improvement projects, even major sporting events. Online education is flexible, but that does not mean it should receive less of your time and attention than a traditional class. By enrolling in an online course, you are making a commitment to the school, to the instructor, to your classmates, and to yourself. Honor that commitment.

- **Allow time for glitches.** It is one thing to finish an assignment at the last minute. It is quite another to *start* at the last minute. The successful online learning experience depends on the combination of a number of components, many of which are beyond your control. You may schedule an all-nighter to write a paper only to find that your Internet connection is down and you are unable to access the online resources you need. Schedule additional "buffer" time into your schedule to accommodate unforeseen speed bumps.

- **Ask for help.** The sooner, the better. Professors appreciate proactive communication. Read the syllabus, create your master calendar, make note of questions and potential problems, then contact your instructor or the appropriate department at the school to find answers and resolve any conflicts. I tell my students that I am much more gracious when they take the initiative to communicate with me ahead of time. Students who miss online discussions and turn in assignments late, *then* ask for my grace, receive very little.

While the online learning process is a two-way street between students and teachers, I am convinced from my own experience as both a student and an instructor that online learning requires additional initiative on the part of the student. Just as students can easily neglect online classes, it is also easy for professors to get caught up in the immediacy of face-to-face, on-campus commitments and classes, and neglect their online commitments. Unfortunately, instructors are not penalized for their slow communication or delayed turnaround of assignments, so responsibility for initiative rests – probably unfairly – on the student more than the instructor.

Again: Discipline yourself. Be proactive. Take responsibility for your commitments and for your own success. Your personal growth is just as much a part of the educational process as the knowledge you receive.

And if you still run into trouble, turn to the next chapter.

STUDENTS SPEAK

"One of the advantages of online education is the flexibility throughout the week; there are few times a person is required to be

online, so the flexibility is phenomenal. However, the significant flexibility also translates into a lack of structure. As an online student, achieving results, writing papers, and making academic progress is even more so your responsibility. As such, online students must create structure for themselves; they must be disciplined in their approach to online education."

"The keys to success for me were to sit down at the start of the semester, examine the assignments, and think through the effort it would take to get them done . . . and plan accordingly."

"Distance learning takes self-motivation, as there is no one to hold your hand. If you need the structure of a weekly class to get things done, distance learning may not be for you. Distance learning means there are a couple of times each year that become insanely busy. The rest of the time is rather delightful."

"Friends and family will continue to vie for your time, and they won't see you attending a physical class, so they may not take the time demands of your class as seriously. Therefore, instead of referring to your classwork as 'homework,' I would recommend viewing 'homework' as 'going to class.' If you tell friends/family you have homework to do, they will likely respond, 'Oh, just do it later. Come spend time with us.' Instead, if you tell friends/family you have to 'go to class,' they will fully understand that you cannot participate in their activity. This small shift in thinking can be a huge help to succeeding in an online program."

"I would recommend – as part of the structure you impose upon yourself – that a student establish certain times throughout the week when they will 'attend class.' Otherwise, it is too easy to procrastinate and rush to finish assignments."

"Prepare yourself. If you can read up on the required reading before the class, do so. Strive to be a good communicator, whether your fellow students do or not. You will get out of this what you put into it. If you see it as a way of getting a degree without too much work you are mistaken. Encourage your fellow students as well as your teachers by giving it 100% of your focus."

PROFESSORS SPEAK

"Students may get even less and even more delayed feedback than in live courses, depending on their instructor, so they need to be self-motivated. They need to follow written instructions carefully, which may be more difficult for oral learners. They need to check and recheck all their course documents, which may be scattered about a Moodle site or its equivalent, to be sure they know everything their instructor may hold them accountable for. They need to pay careful attention to deadlines for assignments and for on-line generated stops. Unlike in a live class, there's no negotiating with the prof or writing that one last paragraph hurriedly if she doesn't yank the paper out of your hand. If it's a time-limited event, the computer will simply stop accepting materials when the second hand goes beyond the time limit."

"The biggest mistakes students make in an online program:
- Getting behind – it's hard to catch up.
- Not asking professors to clarify professor expectations in advance.
- Not realizing (and not planning for) how much time an online class will take.
- Waiting until the last minute to use a technology for the first time – sometimes when the help desk is closed."

"Students need to know that the prof isn't going be 'chasing' them

down with posting deadlines. They need to know that and need to have a good calendar system to note those deadlines at the beginning of the course."

"Students need to make time management decisions. They will not be able to 'add' learning online to an already busy lifestyle."

7. FINDING THE HELP YOU NEED

Quick Reference Resources

My hope is that you will rarely need to refer to this section of the book.

Still, we've seen the various challenges a student can encounter in an online learning environment. This chapter is a place for you to turn if you get stuck. It provides space for you to record your essential course information, followed by a brief troubleshooting guide to walk through in case of a problem.

Begin by recording your essential course and school information using the questions below. If you are using a hard copy of this book, you can write directly on the page or create a separate document for each of your courses. If you are reading this as an e-book, use the questions to create your own data sheet.

Essential Information

Login info:

Username:

Password:

Library info:

Username:

Password:

Name & number of course:

Instructor name (include formal and preferred titles):

Instructor contact information:

Email:

Phone (circle instructor preference):

- Office:
- Home:
- Cell:

Other contact methods:

Best time to contact:

Technical Support contact information:

Email:

Phone:

Support hours:

Other resources (writing center, other important contacts):

Troubleshooting Guide

Sooner or later, you will run into a problem or question during your online studies. When that happens, use the step-by-step guide below to assess the situation and find the help you need.

1. Read the syllabus. Have you read the syllabus completely so that you understand all course requirements and procedures?

2. Familiarize yourself with the course web site. Make sure you know your way around the course site and where to find key areas. Refer back to Chapter 5 for more about "getting familiar" with your course.

3. Ask your classmates for help. They may be experiencing the same problems or may have already found answers. They can encourage you and point you in the right direction.

4. Make a note about what problem or question you are experiencing. Is it a technical issue, or a question about course requirements? In either case, document specifically what you have experienced and what steps you have already taken to try to solve the problem. Don't contact tech support or the instructor until you have made a reasonable attempt to find a solution on your own. But if you're still stuck...

5. Contact the appropriate party. If it's technical support, be ready to explain your problem in detail. Are you having problems logging on? Do you have difficulty accessing parts of the site or your email? When do you experience the problem, and what error messages do you receive?

If your issue pertains to the course components or requirements, contact the instructor. Again, clearly communicate your specific issue or question, and explain what steps you have already taken to find a solution. Provide information about yourself and the course you are taking. Some professors teach hundreds of students; so don't assume they will immediately remember you or your specific situation.

Be sure to utilize the preferred contact method for each individual or department. Then, be patient – especially with instructors – and allow them time to respond. Remember to "allow time for glitches." Meanwhile, work on something you *can* control or access while you are waiting for a solution to the problem at hand.

6. Communicate persistent problems. If the problem seems to be a systemic issue – for example, a problem with how the course is set up, or requirements are communicated, or a recurring technical problem – do your best to help fix the system and reduce the possibility of future recurrence. Assume that instructors and other staff want to know about and rectify recurring issues.

7. Utilize course evaluations. Find out whether you will be provided the opportunity to evaluate the course and your experience at the end of the class term. Provide honest feedback but seek to be helpful even if you have had a negative experience. And if you have enjoyed the course and had a positive experience, be sure to note that as well!

In Conclusion

It is my hope that your experience with online learning is a positive one, and that this book is helpful in making it so. I welcome your stories, comments and suggestions for future revisions of the book; please email me at angie@angieward.net. I look forward to hearing from you, and to incorporating your feedback into the next revision of this book.

References

Chapter 1

1. I. Elaine Allen and Jeff Seaman, *Changing Course: Ten Years of Tracking Online Education in the United States*, Babson Survey Research Group and Quahog Research Group, LLC, 2013.

2. Scott Jaschik, "MOOC Mess," www.insidehighered.coml, Feb. 4, 2013, http://www.insidehighered.com/news/2013/02/04/cours era-forced-call-mooc-amid-complaints-about-course.

3 I. Elaine Allen and Jeff Seaman, *Going the Distance: Online Education in the United States, 2011*, Babson Survey Research Group, 2011, 5.

4. "Baker's Guide to Christian Online Learning," http://www.bakersguide.com. Accessed February 26, 2013.

5. Angie Ward, "Back to School," *Leadership,* Vol. 32 No. 4 (Fall 2011), 93-96.

Chapter 2

1. USPTO Patent Full-Text and Image Database, http://patft.uspto.gov/netacgi/nph-Parser?Sect1=PTO1&Sect2=HITOFF&d=PALL&p=1&u=%2Fnetahtml%2FPTO%2Fsrchnum.htm&r=1&f=G&l=50&s1=6988138.PN.&OS=PN/6988138&RS=PN/698813 8. Accessed February 26, 2013.

2. I. Elaine Allen and Jeff Seaman, *Changing Course: Ten Years of Tracking Online Education in the United States,* Babson Survey Research Group and Quahog Research Group, LLC, 2013, 4.

3. I. Elaine Allen and Jeff Seaman, *Going the Distance: Online Education in the United States, 2011*, Babson Survey Research Group, 2011, 7.

4. "The Trouble with Online College," *The New York Times*, February 18, 2013, http://www.nytimes.com/2013/02/19/opinion/the-trouble-with-online-college.html?_r=1&. Accessed March 1, 2013.

Chapter 3

1. "The Database of Accredited Postsecondary Institutions and Programs," U.S. Department of Education, http://ope.ed.gov/accreditation/. Accessed March 1, 2013.

Acknowledgements

Thanks to the many students and colleagues who shared their insights and experiences with online learning for this book. You know who you are, and I am grateful for your willing and honest contributions.

Thanks to the educational institutions that have given me the opportunity to design and teach their online, hybrid, and traditional courses. I am grateful for your confidence and trust.

Thanks to the professors who first gave me a love of learning and a passion for teaching. It is an honor to now be considered your colleague.

Thanks to all the fantastic students I have had the privilege of getting to know through my classes. It is always an honor to journey with you.

Most importantly, thanks to my wonderful husband and sons for their unconditional love and support. Love to you always.

Appendix: Students and Professors Speak

More Wisdom From Those Who Have Been There

So many students and professors submitted their thoughts regarding online learning that there was not enough room to include all of it in the body of the book. Following are additional comments in response to survey questions.

STUDENTS SPEAK

What do you wish you had known before you started your course or program?

"One issue I've seen with students is that they are not prepared for the amount of time and life disruption caused by online courses. Schools sell online course with the idea of convenience. There is nothing convenient about education, and online courses in some ways take more time than face-to-face."

What would you tell an incoming distance education student?

"Be thankful that these options exist! They are a great way to continue with life and pursue a degree."

"You really have to set aside set time for reading, and make it a strong habit!"

"Stay the course. There will be times when you want to give up. Don't!"

"Put everything into your studies. Read your books. Find out what else the authors have written."

"I would encourage students to stick with their particular program and to not give up. At times life gets hectic and when you add in schoolwork, it's easy to think that you can't handle it. My advice would be to look ahead at the bigger picture and remember that no matter how tough things may seem, in the end getting their degree is well worth the struggle and the personal sacrifices made along the way."

What, in your experience, are keys to student success in an online program?

"The key to success is time management. Creating calendars for assignments and deadlines; creating 'tickle notes' to pop up throughout the week as reminders; setting aside reading time and study time; using alarm clocks to move through assignments; physically going to the library or some external place to study and write; saving back-up copies of your work to flash drives; acknowledging your family support as you go through the process."

"Perseverance. Personal interest in the topic. Support of family and friends."

"Get to know your professors. Find out their expectations. Always try to go one step further, one step faster than they ask for things. This will create trust, and you will get a good grade. The professors hold the keys to the car."

What did you enjoy the most about your online program?

"I enjoyed the variety of materials I read, as they caused me to think differently and more deeply about what was presented. The reading was very stimulating and challenging."

"My cohort was enjoyable and I've maintained those relationships beyond class. The online experience help create a deeper bond and sense of camaraderie among our group. "

What was the hardest part of your online program?

"Keeping on schedule with the readings."

"Traveling the distance to meet (12 hours driving)."

"By far the hardest part of the program was communication. In residential and more traditional education models, the student has a lot of interaction time with faculty. There's the value of proximity, the advantage of being on campus and interacting with the staff/faculty, and the access to school resources (library, facilities, etc.). In the online/hybrid model, all communication is dependent on answering emails or returning phone calls. To be honest, there have been more than a few times that I've wondered if my email was ignored, deleted, or sent to the spam folder. However, there is also a freedom in that because I can send emails any time of day or night, and I may get answers outside of traditional office hours. But when needs are pressing, I've learned I can't be in a hurry."

"Finding suitable internet connections on the road (my job involves traveling)."

"Motivation and time management. As someone with young children who was beginning and leading a new company, the flexibility of the program was great. However, there were times I wanted to give up because it was a very busy season of my life."

"The video courses in my program felt sterile. Camera angles weren't horrible, but they were such that it didn't draw you into the class. You felt like you were observing from the hall through a window."

"Deciding to start and securing funds to pay for the classes."

"I had difficulty absorbing what I was reading. By this I mean processing the information from the multitude of books, articles, and journals we read. I read them, but did not feel that I had digested the information sufficiently for deep learning to occur. As a consequence, I have a shallow understanding of many elements but have not internalized all that I 'learned'."

Any other thoughts or advice you would give to others who are embarking on an online learning experience?

"Jump in with both feet, as the pace is fast. Try to stay ahead of the game so you have completed presentations or papers a bit early as it lessens the stress of the program."

"Keep engaged with the online dialogues and don't be afraid to speak up and argue with others as defending your positions and thoughts are also part of the learning process."

"Do it before you get too old. If you're too old, do it anyway."

"Come to class as a student/learner, not an expert. Schools are a place to acquire knowledge, not demonstrate knowledge."

"It is the wave of the future; embrace it."

PROFESSORS SPEAK

What do students who are going to take an online course or program need to know for the best success?

"Students need to make time management decisions. They will not be able to 'add' learning online to an already busy lifestyle."

"Many students are used to a system where they've become overly dependent on their instructors to pull them along in the learning process. Online courses can be a real wake-up call because they require the learner to be self-directed. The successful online student is always a self-disciplined student."

What are the biggest mistakes students make in this kind of class or program?

"Thinking they will be able to learn the computer skills without effort. Even young adults will have to practice with the platform."

"Alienating peers or instructors by flaming (bashing and insulting)."

"The biggest mistake, by far, that online students make is they miss the opportunity to engage their professor. If you want more feedback on your paper, then ask for it. If you want specific feedback on a specific part of your paper (citations, a particular idea, or a piece that you think is strong or weak), then email and ask for it. When you run into difficulties or confusion, send your professor an email, or better yet, send out an email to your fellow students."

About the Author

Angie Ward, Ph.D. is a leadership teacher, writer and coach. She has designed and taught residential, online, and hybrid courses in undergraduate, graduate, and professional leadership education programs around the United States. Angie lives outside Indianapolis with her husband, two sons, and one very spoiled beagle. For more information about the author and her work, visit www.angieward.net.